If you were a

Prefix

Copilot

by Marcie Aboff
illustrated by Sara Gray

PICTURE WINDOW BOOKS
Minneapolis, Minnesota

prefix a letter or group of letters placed before a word to change its meaning

Editor: Christianne Jones
Designer: Hilary Wacholz
Page Production: Melissa Kes
Art Director: Nathan Gassman
The illustrations in this book were created with acrylics.

Picture Window Books
151 Good Counsel Drive
P.O. Box 669
Mankato, MN 56002-0669
877-845-8392
www.picturewindowbooks.com

Printed in the United States of America.

All books published by Picture
Window Books are manufactured
with paper containing at least
10 percent post-consumer waste.

**Library of Congress Cataloging-in-
Publication Data**
Aboff, Marcie.
If you were a prefix / by Marcie Aboff ;
illustrated by Sara Gray.
p. cm. — (Word fun)
Includes index.
ISBN-13: 978-1-4048-4773-6 (library binding)
ISBN-13: 978-1-4048-4777-4 (paperback)
1. English language—Suffixes and prefixes—
Juvenile literature. I. Gray, Sara, ill. II. Title.
PE1175.A23 2008
428.1—dc22   2008006347

Looking for prefixes?

Watch for the underlined letters
throughout the book.

Special thanks to our advisers for their expertise:

Rosemary G. Palmer, Ph.D., Department of Literacy
College of Education, Boise State University

Terry Flaherty, Ph.D., Professor of English
Minnesota State University, Mankato

If you were a prefix ...

3

... you would come first!

4

Prefixes can make a regular school a <u>pre</u>school, change angles, to <u>tri</u>angles, and make lucky <u>un</u>lucky.

If you were a prefix, you would be a letter or group of letters placed before a word to change its meaning.

The colorful caterpillar <u>trans</u>formed into a <u>multi</u>colored butterfly.

If you were the prefix "re," you could do things over again.

During the <u>re</u>match, the giraffe <u>re</u>bounded the ball and dribbled down the path.

8

The monkey had to **re**play the phone message about **re**placing the missing bananas.

If you were the prefix "co," you could help do an important job.

The <u>co</u>pilot helped the pilot fly the airplane.

The <u>co</u>-captain helped the captain steer the ship.

If you were the prefix "tele," you could talk to, see, and watch things far away.

The owl called the eagle on the <u>tele</u>phone.

The robin looked for the eagle with a <u>tele</u>scope.

The birds watched their favorite show on <u>television</u>!

13

If you were a prefix, you could give a word added meaning.

The jaguar looked like a star driving his ordinary car.

The jaguar looked like a superstar driving his extraordinary car.

15

If you were a prefix, you could change the same word in different ways.

You could make a cycle a <u>uni</u>cycle, a <u>bi</u>cycle, or a <u>tri</u>cycle.

17

If you were a prefix, you could change a word to mean its opposite.

The happy rabbit jumped out of the hole, and his friends appeared.

The <u>un</u>happy rabbit climbed into the hole, and his friends <u>dis</u>appeared.

If you were a prefix, you could be yourself. The prefix *pre* means "before." The word *fix* means "to place." *Prefix* means "to place before."

21

FUN WITH PREFIXES

Cut out 14 pieces of paper. On each piece of paper, write one of the prefixes or root words from below. Mix them up and see if you can put the words back together. Then make your own list and have a friend match the words. You can even time each other and see who can match the words faster.

mis place
un finished
non sense
mid way
pre view
tele cast
over work

Glossary

extraordinary—more than ordinary

multicolored—having many colors

prefix—a letter or group of letters placed before a word to change its meaning

rebounded—to gain possession of the basketball after a shot

root—the basic meaning of the word

transformed—changed form

To Learn More

More Books to Read

Draze, Dianne. *Red Hot Root Words*. Austin, Tex.: Dandy Lion Publications, 2003.

Heinrichs, Ann. *Prefixes and Suffixes*. Chanhassen, Minn.: Child's World, 2006.

Langton, Charan. *Big Words for Little Kids*. San Ramon, Calif.: Mountcastle Company, 2007.

On the Web

FactHound offers a safe, fun way to find Web sites related to topics in this book. All of the sites on FactHound have been researched by our staff.

1. Visit www.facthound.com
2. Type in this special code: 1404847731
3. Click on the FETCH IT button.

Your trusty FactHound will fetch the best sites for you!

Index

Look for all of the books in the Word Fun series:

11/08